The SUSAN B. ANTHONY You Never Knew

BY JAMES LINCOLN COLLIER

Children's Press®
A Division of Scholastic Inc.
New York Toronto London Auckland Sydney
Mexico City New Delhi Hong Kong
Danbury, Connecticut

Library of Congress Cataloging-in-Publication Data

Collier, James Lincoln, 1928-
  The Susan B. Anthony you never knew / James Lincoln Collier.
      p. cm.
  Includes bibliographical references and index.
  ISBN 0-516-24428-0
  1. Anthony, Susan B. (Susan Brownell), 1820-1906—Juvenile literature. 2.
Feminists—United States—Biography—Juvenile literature. 3. Suffragists—
United States—Biography—Juvenile literature. I. Title.
  HQ1413.A55C563 2004
  305.42'092—dc22

                                      2003028306

Illustrations by Greg Copeland
Book design by A. Natacha Pimentel C.

Photographs © 2004: Art Resource, NY: 35, 66 (National Portrait Gallery, Smith-
sonian Institution), 63, 73, 76 bottom (Snark); Corbis Images: 7, 15, 17, 31, 36,
45, 50, 56, 59, 76 top, 76 center (Bettmann), 71 (Rice), 20 (Napolean
Sarony/Bettmann), 46 (S.A. Taylor), 12, 28, 40, 49, 53, 60, 69; Culver Pictures/Sy
Seidman Collection: cover, 4; Hulton|Archive/Getty Images: 9, 11, 25, 42, 75;
Library of Congress: 1 (Sara J. Eddy), 32, 72.

CONTENTS

Chapter 1

A SERIOUS UPBRINGING

PROBABLY NO MOVEMENT OF THE PAST 150 years has changed life for Americans as much as what we call feminism—the fight for female rights. Today not only grown women but also girls can do many things that their grandmothers rarely dared, and their great-grandmothers had never even dreamed of doing. A hundred years ago a properly brought-up girl had to wear many layers of clothing that kept most of her body covered. Such clothes made it hard for her to run and jump, much less play sports.

Susan B. Anthony, in 1848, when she was starting to become interested in women's issues.

She couldn't wear shorts or blue jeans. She could not sit with her legs crossed, wave her arms around, wrestle with boys or even with girls.

Girls could not play rough sports like baseball and hockey. They were sometimes scolded for laughing loudly or shouting. As women, they could not vote in most states, nor become senators or mayors. Women doctors and lawyers were rare, although there were a few. Only a small percentage of women went to college.

Farther back, let us say 150 years ago, around the time of the Civil War, women were almost always legally ruled by men—first their fathers and then, their husbands. At that time a married woman could not have money or own property, let alone vote. Even if she earned money with her own hands, it belonged to her husband, who could do whatever he wanted with it.

During one of her lecture tours, Susan B. Anthony went into a tavern run by a young wife. While caring for her baby, the wife served a supper to Susan, who described the scene as follows:

. . . *beautiful white bread, butter, cheese, pickles, apple and mince pie, and excellent peach preserves. She gave us her warm bedroom to sleep in, and on a row of pegs hung the loveliest embroidered petticoat and baby clothes, all the work of that young woman's fingers. . . . She prepared a 6 o'clock breakfast for us, fried pork, mashed potatoes, mince pie, and for me, at my especial request, a plate of delicious baked sweet apples and a pitcher of rich milk. Now for the moral of this story: When we came to pay our bill, the dolt of a husband took the money and put it in his pocket. He had not lifted a hand to lighten that woman's burdens . . . yet the law gives him the right to every dollar she earns. . . .*

The woman's suffrage movement of the 19th century got a great deal of attention from the press. This illustration was drawn for an article in the respected magazine Harper's Bazaar, *and shows suffragettes in a serious manner.*

Even worse, a woman had no rights over her own children. Husbands could make all the decisions about them—how they were to be raised, where they would go to school, and everything else. A husband could even send the children away to live someplace else, no matter what his wife thought about it. And no matter how badly a husband treated his wife, it was almost impossible for the wife to get a divorce if the husband didn't want her to.

Today, as we know, the situation for women is far different. More females than males go to college. There are plenty of female lawyers and doctors, as well as female airline pilots, bus drivers, and police officers. Indeed, there are women in almost every kind of job and profession. Girls today play every sport that boys do. There are now professional leagues for women in many sports, like basketball and soccer. Women not only vote, but run for every type of public office. And not only do women control their own property, they also run large businesses.

It is true, of course, that life for males has changed a lot over the past 150 years. But the change to the lives of females has been much greater. Much of the improvement of things for women was created by the feminists of the twentieth century, most of whom are alive today.

But the foundation for it all was laid by a remarkable group of women in the nineteenth century, among them Lucretia Mott, Elizabeth Cady Stanton, Carrie Chapman Catt, and Lucy Stone. The most important of them all was Susan B. Anthony. Without her there is no doubt that women would not have come as far as they have today.

Susan B. Anthony was born in 1820. Her family was Quaker. This was, and is, a serious religion. In Susan's day Quakers did not allow themselves to drink alcohol, to dance, to wear fancy clothes, to waste time

Although some reports on the suffrage movement were sympathetic, the majority were hostile. This cartoon suggests that women were not merely interested in gaining the vote, but wanted to dominate men as well.

in frivolity. But, surprisingly, the Quakers allowed women more rights than many other religions did. True, they believed that a woman's place was in the home, not in business or politics. But they believed that before God women were the equals of men. Women were allowed to speak up at Quaker meetings, which they often could not do in other churches. They sometimes held important jobs in Quaker communities and could even preach.

On top of that, Susan's parents were more open-minded than most Quakers. Her mother had not been born a Quaker. As a girl she had loved dancing and dressing in colorful clothes. Susan's father had been told he mustn't marry a woman who wasn't a Quaker, but he married Susan's mother anyway. She had to give up dancing and pretty clothes when she married Susan's father, but she was never truly a Quaker at heart. So Susan B. Anthony had independent-minded parents. She grew up to be independent-minded herself.

The Anthonys had six children, four girls and two boys. In those days schools were very crude. At the time many Americans never learned to read and write. Girls particularly did not get much schooling. Why bother educating girls, when they were to become wives and mothers? Better for them to learn how to

Most religions did not allow women to preach. However, the Quakers expected women to speak out at their religious meetings, as one woman is doing in this picture. Susan B. Anthony was used to hearing women express themselves in public.

make jam, churn butter, pluck chickens, and obey their husbands than to learn to read and write.

Quakers, however, believed in education. Susan's parents wanted all their children educated, including the girls. When Susan's father discovered that the local teacher did not know how to do long division, he hired teachers to come to the house.

He could afford to do so, because he was growing wealthy from some mills he owned, first in Massachusetts and then in Battenville, New York. Susan B. Anthony began life with a better education than most girls of her time got. As a teenager, her father sent her away to a school where she studied literature and philosophy as well as algebra and geography.

At this school she met a young woman named Lydia Mott. Lydia was a relative of an older woman named Lucretia Mott. Lucretia was one of the rare female lecturers who gave talks on many important subjects of the time. Once Lucretia came to lecture near Susan's school. Susan was very impressed by Lucretia Mott. She was interested to see a woman doing things only men were supposed to do.

Lucretia Mott was one of the first American feminist leaders. She and Elizabeth Cady Stanton organized the now legendary Seneca Falls conference, which started the American feminist movement.

In the late 1830s hard times struck American businesses. Susan's father lost not only most of his money, but the mills that he owned, too. Susan now had to earn money to help the family. About the only type of job open to women, aside from factory work, was teaching. Susan went to New Rochelle, New York, and later other places, to teach. For fifteen years she was a schoolteacher. She later told a newspaper reporter:

> *I wasn't a bit timid. I was only fifteen, but I thought I was the wisest girl in all the world. I knew it all. No one could make me think anything else. . . . I recall one pupil I had. I was very young at the time. I had been warned that he had put the last master out of the window and that he would surely insult me. I went into that school boy when he began on me. I made him take off his coat and I gave him a good whipping with a stout switch. . . . As I got older I abolished whipping. If I couldn't manage a child I thought it was my ignorance, my lack of ability as a teacher. I always felt less the woman when I struck a blow. . . .*

Susan was a good teacher, but she realized that no matter how good she became she would never be paid as much as male teachers. People believed that men had to support families and needed good salaries but that women teachers would be supported by their fathers or their husbands.

This seemed unjust to Susan. She had been raised in a family where women were allowed to speak out. She was sure that women were just as smart and capable as men. Once she told a relative that she was studying algebra. Later, at dinner, she served this man some wonderful

biscuits she had made. He said, "I'd rather see a woman make biscuits like these than solve the knottiest problem in algebra."

Susan replied, "There is no reason why she should not be able to do both."

Susan was coming to resent the power men had over women, but she had not yet figured out what to do about it. The idea of a woman fighting against the authority of men would have seemed strange, even hateful, at the time. But she had a restless mind. She wanted to be active in events. She decided to join the temperance movement—the fight against drunkenness.

At the time people drank more wine, beer, and whiskey than people do today. Many children were allowed to have beer or "hard" cider

Before about 1830, Americans routinely drank a good deal more alcohol than they do today. Most did not overdo it, but some did. There were problems with husbands drinking up their wages or abusing their wives when drunk. By the 1830s a movement to curb drinking was growing. This picture shows the song sheet for a song about the drinking problem.

with their meals. Unfortunately, men often spent too much of their wages on drinking, leaving their families to go hungry. Sometimes drunken husbands and fathers would abuse their wives and children. Of course there were also women who drank too much, but mainly the problem was with men.

As a result, many women believed that temperance was something they should fight for. Susan decided to get into this fight. She very quickly discovered that the temperance organizations were run by men. Women were welcome at temperance meetings and could help with the work, but men were in charge and did the talking at the meetings.

However, by the 1840s, when Susan was in her twenties, a few daring women had started their own temperance organizations. Susan joined one of these. Few of the women in it could be persuaded to get up on a platform to speak, for it was considered unlady-like to do so. But Susan had grown up going to Quaker meetings where women often spoke. So one day she came into a meeting hall where two hundred temperance workers had gathered. With a speech in hand, she climbed onto the platform and in a firm voice told the women at the meeting that it was up to them to do something about the abuse of alcohol.

Men were generally the leaders of the temperance movement, but many people believed that it was wives who suffered most from drinking. As a result, women became strong crusaders for temperance, as this cartoon shows.

Women should stop serving beer and wine at their dinner parties. They should object to men who came to their parties drunk. "Ladies! There is no neutral position for us to assume."

According to one historian, "The next day the village buzzed with talk of the meeting; only a few criticized Susan for speaking in public, and almost all agreed that she was the smartest woman [in their town]."

One day in 1848 she read in her newspaper about a meeting that had been held in the little town of Seneca Falls, in upstate New York, not far from where Susan was living then. At the Seneca Falls meeting a declaration of women's rights, modeled on the Declaration of Independence, had been discussed and voted on. The meeting made big news in papers across the country.

Soon she heard about a second meeting devoted to women's rights. This one was held in Rochester, one of the biggest cities upstate. Susan's parents had gone to it. They had come home very impressed by the woman who had organized it, Mrs. Elizabeth Cady Stanton. Susan decided she would like to meet Mrs. Stanton.

But Susan was busy with her teaching and her temperance work. She had no time to travel. Then, in 1851, she happened to go to a meeting in Seneca Falls. As she walked from the meeting with a friend she was staying with, they came across Elizabeth Cady Stanton. The two women were introduced.

Elizabeth Stanton wrote later, "There she stood with her good earnest face and genial smile, dressed in gray silk, hat and all the same color, relieved with pale blue ribbons, the perfection of neatness and sobriety. I liked her thoroughly." It was the most fateful meeting in the history of American women.

Chapter 2

THE GREAT FRIENDSHIP

WE CANNOT TALK ABOUT SUSAN B. Anthony without discussing Elizabeth Cady Stanton. For many years these two women were a team, fighting together to improve life for women. They were in many ways different. Susan was quieter, a planner, a good politician and strategist. She did much of the thinking and planning for the women's movement.

Elizabeth was the emotional, enthusiastic one. She married, had seven children, and was very much a mother and homemaker.

Elizabeth Cady Stanton (left) with Susan in 1881. By this time they had been working together for womens' rights for almost thirty years.

Indeed, as she aged, she grew to look like everybody's idea of a wonderful grandmother, gray-haired and plump. But no matter how motherly she appeared, she was a determined fighter for women's rights. Of the two, she was by far the best speaker. She could be passionate, but she could also tell good stories to get audiences on her side. People always loved to hear Elizabeth Cady Stanton speak.

Elizabeth was born in 1815, the fourth child in a family of six children in Johnstown, in upstate New York. Her father was a very successful lawyer and politician who even became a congressman.

Her mother was from a wealthy and well-known family. She was nearly six feet tall, very tall for the time, and was quite strong-minded. Elizabeth grew up feeling that her mother didn't like her very much. This was probably not true, but it is true that Elizabeth's mother demanded a lot of her children. They had to be well-behaved, go to church often, always do what they were told without arguing. Sometimes Elizabeth grew fearful and had bad dreams. At other times she was rebellious and fought with her mother.

She got along much better with her father. He sometimes backed her up when she refused to do what her mother wanted her to do. When her mother had

had enough of Elizabeth's rebelliousness, she would send her down to her father's law office to be disciplined. Instead of giving her a talking to, her father would let her sit and listen to the conversations in the law office.

Once, when Elizabeth was a little girl, she heard the story of a local woman named Flora Campbell, whom her family knew. Flora had made some money selling farm produce, like milk and eggs. With the profits she bought her own farm. However, according to the law, the farm belonged to her husband, even though Flora had paid for it.

When her husband died, he left the farm to their son. The son was very wasteful of money and did not take care of the farm. Flora decided she had better get the farm back. She went to see Elizabeth's father. Sadly, he told her that there was nothing he could do. The laws were against her. When Elizabeth heard this story she decided to cut those laws out of her father's law books. He explained that removing the laws from his books would not change anything. But maybe when she was grown, she might try to change the laws. And that is what she did.

By the time she was eleven, Elizabeth had decided that in order to be independent, she had to do the things that boys could do. She learned to be a good horsewoman and studied hard subjects like Greek. In 1830, when she was fifteen, she went off to a girls' boarding school in Troy, near Albany, New York.

Many girls' schools were aimed at teaching girls good manners and how to dress well. But this school was run by a woman named Emma Willard, who felt that girls were entitled to a serious education. At this school Elizabeth was drilled in writing. She said later that her great skill with words began here.

She graduated from the Troy school in 1833. She was not yet interested in any cause, but that would come soon. In these years, beginning about 1820, a great many "movements" were starting in America. The nation was, at the time, a rough place. People drank a great amount of liquor, as we have seen. Houses were not particularly clean and tidy, nor were the people who lived in them. Most people only took a bath once a week. Many people gambled too much, betting on card games or horse races. The majority of Americans did not go to church regularly. People spit wherever they were. Pigs and dogs wandered into churches.

By about 1820 many Americans thought it was time for a change, that the country should be reformed. People were drawn to various causes. Many became interested in reviving the true spirit of Christianity.

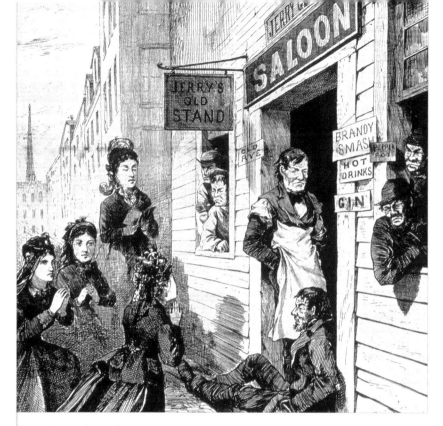

Crusaders for temperance often went into saloons to pray for the drinkers, hoping to embarrass them into leaving. When they were barred from entry, they sometimes prayed outside, as shown in this picture.

There were revival meetings everywhere. Preachers went around the countryside persuading people to live like Christians, and many decided to do so. Others were interested in temperance, and hoped to get people to drink less. Some were touched by the suffering of black slaves, most of them in the South, and started the abolitionist movement to abolish slavery in the

United States. There were other causes as well. But there was not yet a women's movement.

These movements were not always in agreement about what reforms were most important or how to get them, but they had a lot in common. They all wanted a cleaner, more decent America. They wanted Americans to think of what was good for their families and their communities, not just about themselves. They all believed that women were purer, more moral than men. Because of this idea, women saw that they could be important to several of these movements.

Two people interested in the reform movements of the time were cousins of Elizabeth, named Gerrit and Ann Smith. Elizabeth's family often visited the Smiths in the little town of Peterboro, New York. Elizabeth always enjoyed these visits because there were dancing, games, and laughter. The Smiths belonged to both the temperance and abolition movements. On her visits to the Smith house Elizabeth joined in the debates and conversations about the reform movements.

And it was there, in 1839, that she met a man named Henry Brewster Stanton. He was an ardent abolitionist and had been attacked by mobs of men who were against rights for African Americans. Very quickly Elizabeth and Henry fell in love, and in May 1840 they were married.

For their wedding trip they went to London, where Henry was to speak at the Anti-Slavery Convention. Women were welcome to join many of these antislavery societies, but in most of them they were not expected to speak—indeed, they were not to do anything but applaud the male speakers.

In London Elizabeth met some women who were determined to take active parts in the meetings. One of them was Lucretia Mott. Elizabeth and Lucretia quickly formed a friendship. They made plans to speak at the meeting, but they were not permitted to do so. Instead the women were told that they must sit in special seats at one end of the hall. Elizabeth and Lucretia were very angry at such treatment. They began talking about having a women's rights convention when they got back home.

We must understand how brave and unusual this idea was. From time to time in the past there were a few women, such as the Englishwoman Mary Wollstonecraft, who had spoken out about greater rights for women. But women had never united as a group to demand more rights.

Elizabeth and Lucretia did nothing about their idea for several years. Probably they were nervous about it. But it is also true that Elizabeth had a growing family.

She and Henry settled in Boston where Elizabeth raised her children and worked for the abolitionist and temperance movements when she had time. In Boston she made the first of the many thousands of public speeches she would give in her life. But it was about temperance, not aimed at gaining women's rights.

In 1847 Henry and Elizabeth decided to move their family to the small town of Seneca Falls, New York. The damp climate of Boston was not good for Henry, who was having problems with his lungs. They believed that the air in upstate New York would be better for him.

After Boston, Seneca Falls seemed tame to Elizabeth. She wanted to be active in movements and causes. As it happened, in 1848 Lucretia Mott came to visit a relative in a town near Seneca Falls.

Susan B. Anthony never married, but Elizabeth Cady Stanton did and raised a large family. She still found time for her feminist activities. Here she is shown with her daughter Harriet.

She and Elizabeth got together. They quickly revived the idea of a convention for women's rights. They persuaded a few other local women to join in. They decided to hold their convention in July. Although Lucretia was twenty years older and much more experienced in public affairs, Elizabeth took the lead. With the help of others, she drew up the famous list of grievances modeled on the Declaration of Independence. They publicized the convention in the local papers.

They did not expect much of a turnout. However, three hundred people came. Startled by the size of the crowd, when Elizabeth rose to speak she felt like "suddenly abandoning all her principles and running away." But she spoke eloquently, presenting the list of women's demands. There were many of them. Women should be paid as much as men for doing the same jobs. They should be able to own their own property. They should be able to go to college and join the professions. Elizabeth presented these demands to the meeting, and then she added one more: the right for women to vote.

This demand started a furor. All the other rights on the list passed the convention easily. The demand for suffrage—the right to vote—only barely squeaked by. For many women, asking for the right to vote was going too far. Still, the majority were for it.

Much to the surprise of Elizabeth and the others, the women's rights convention at Seneca Falls caused a sensation in newspapers all across the nation. The men who wrote and edited the papers disliked much about the list of rights demanded by the convention, but the demand for the vote was the one that bothered them the most. They said that giving women the vote would drag them into the dirty world of politics, that women were too pure for that. They said that women were too emotional to think clearly about politics and would be easily swayed by slick politicians. They said that if women went into politics their homes would suffer, and their children would be neglected. They said that women were already well cared for by their husbands and had all the rights they needed.

Elizabeth said later that if she had known how much uproar the women's rights convention would cause she might not have called it. A lot of women who had signed the declaration took their signatures back. One of them was Elizabeth's sister, whose father and husband demanded that she do so.

But Elizabeth would not back down. Instead she called the second meeting at Rochester, the one that Susan B. Anthony's parents went to. Despite her family responsibilities, Elizabeth Cady Stanton was off and running.

An artist's version of Elizabeth speaking at the legendary Seneca Falls convention in 1848

The meeting in the little town of Seneca Falls in 1848 was the start of the women's movement of the nineteenth century. Everything that has happened since can be traced back to that moment. Many women made it happen, but the first shove came from Lucretia Mott and Elizabeth Cady Stanton.

"Failure is impossible!"

Susan B. Anthony

Chapter 3

THE GREAT WORK BEGINS

N O MATTER HOW IMPORTANT Elizabeth Cady Stanton was in getting the women's movement started, in the end it was Susan B. Anthony who became the driving force behind it. One important factor was that most of the other women in the movement got married and had children. Susan did not. She could devote all of her time to feminist causes, and after her meeting with Elizabeth in 1851, she did.

Susan B. Anthony's final words to the National American Woman's Sufferage Association. The slogan, "Failure is Impossible," is still used by feminists today.

Money, of course, was always a problem. But by this time her father's businesses had improved. Susan could go home when she needed a place to stay for awhile.

Later in life many people asked Susan why she never got married. Many men who opposed women's rights said she was angry with men because nobody wanted to marry her. Newspapers called her "a slab-sided spinster [who] . . . failed to get a whole man" and a "grim Old Gal with a manly air."

However, several men did ask Susan to marry them. She turned them all down. We are not sure why. We must remember that in those days it was unusual for a woman not to marry. Over the years Susan gave several reasons for staying single. As a girl, she recalled, "I never cared for little boys. I was much too serious. And I am sure they were not interested in me. Why, I wouldn't have left my book for one of them."

Another time she said, "It always happened that the men I wanted were those I could not get, and those who wanted me I wouldn't have." She also said, "I never found the man who was necessary to my happiness. I was very well as I was." And she added, "I'm sure no man could have made me any happier than I have been."

These statements were no doubt all true. Susan thought that women were not just as good as men, but better than them in many ways. She said, "I would not object to marriage if it were not that women throw away every plan and purpose of their own life, to conform to the plans and purposes of the man's life." That is probably the heart of it. Married women of the time did not have much freedom. And the one thing Susan B. Anthony would never give up was her freedom.

Quickly Susan and Elizabeth grew close to each other. Soon Elizabeth introduced Susan to another woman determined to fight for women's rights, Lucy Stone. Lucy had been raised on a farm doing the hard,

Lucy Stone became an important part of the feminist leadership around Susan. She was one of the first women to insist on keeping her own name when she married.

drudging work. She wanted to make more of herself, however. She studied whenever she could and managed to get into Oberlin College, the first college in the

United States to take women. She joined the abolitionist movement to free the slaves, but everywhere she went she talked about women's rights, too. When she married she refused to take her husband's name, but insisted on being called Lucy Stone. She soon developed a friendship with Susan and Elizabeth. One historian says that this friendship of Susan B. Anthony, Elizabeth Cady Stanton, and Lucy Stone "developed the women's rights movement in the United States."

Even so, the three women were not ready to plunge headfirst into women's rights. They continued to work at other causes, particularly temperance, which they saw as important for women. Susan belonged to a group called the Daughters of Temperance, which had been started by women. She was used to speaking at meetings of this organization.

In an effort to shame drinkers, these women sat in a barroom taking down the names of men there. In the rear a man is turning loose a skunk in the hopes of driving the women away.

Then one evening she went to a meeting of a male organization, the Sons of Temperance. At this meeting she spoke up during a debate. Men were astonished that a woman would dare to speak at one of their meetings. The chairman said, "The sisters were not invited here to speak, but to listen and to learn."

Susan was angry. She soon learned that there would be a third women's rights convention in Syracuse, New York, in 1852. She went and talked with many women who were determined to push for women's rights. Susan was caught up in their feelings. These new friends immediately saw Susan's abilities. She was elected secretary of the convention. One historian says, "Never before had she heard so many earnest, intelligent women plead so convincingly for property rights, civil rights, and the ballot. Never before had she seen so clearly that in a republic women as well as men should enjoy these rights. The ballot assumed a new importance for her. Her conversion to woman suffrage was complete."

The next year she went to a state teachers' convention in Rochester. Two-thirds of the teachers there were women, but once again the men did all the talking. Impatiently Susan sat there, listening. She was now committed to demanding rights for women. She rose and called out, "Mr. Chairman." The historian says: "At the sound of a woman's voice, an astonished rustle of excitement swept through the audience, and when the chairman . . . had recovered from his surprise, he patronizingly asked, 'What will the lady have?' Susan said 'I wish, sir, to speak to the subject under discussion.'" If she had been a man, there would have been no question about speaking. But the chairman decided to put it to a vote. There was a long debate about whether women ought to be allowed to speak. Finally it was voted by a small majority that Susan could speak. So intelligent were her comments that several men came up and congratulated her. But that was not the majority opinion. When the chairman was later asked why no women ever lectured at the teachers' convention or were put on committees, he said that he would not think of dragging them in the dust by doing such work.

Susan saw clearly that if women were to get any-where they could not depend on male reformers. She began now to organize speaking tours for herself, not only around New York State, but elsewhere in the country, too. At a time when there was no television, no movies, radio, or recorded music, going to lectures was an important form of entertainment. Some popular speakers aimed only to be interesting or funny. Famous writers like Mark Twain and the Englishman Charles Dickens worked up amusing lectures for the purpose of making money. Other lecturers would describe their adventures in foreign lands or fascinating sights they had seen, like the Swiss Alps or the Amazon River.

But many speakers lectured on politics or social issues of the day. Such lectures might be two or three hours long. People who went to them ended up knowing more about the great questions of the time

This picture was probably drawn to accompany a magazine article about the feminist movement. It shows Susan, right, and another feminist leader being escorted to a speaker's platform in Cincinnati. The activities of the feminist leaders like Susan, Elizabeth, and Lucy Stone got much attention from newspapers and magazines.

than do many people today who quickly gulp down the television news before turning to the latest quiz show or comedy.

Women's rights was a very controversial subject, and people were interested in hearing about it. There was a practical reason for Susan to lecture, too. Women like Lucy Stone and Elizabeth Stanton had husbands to support them. Susan had to earn her own money. Somehow she had to have a living if she were to work for women's rights. She could earn fees for giving lectures. She could also make money selling pamphlets she published about women's rights to members of her audiences. She did not earn much money in this way, but she could earn enough to keep herself going.

Writing her own lectures forced Susan to think deeply and clearly about women's rights. She began to see that one very basic problem had to do with marriage laws and customs. For a long time it had been the rule that when a woman married she became almost part of her husband, like his hand or his foot. She had no separate self apart from him. Her money was his, her body was his. She could no more get a divorce from him than his foot could get a divorce, unless he agreed. Of course, many marriages were good, and many husbands did not take advantage of their wives. But there were bad husbands who abused their wives. It was very difficult for those wives to escape their husbands.

Susan and Elizabeth decided they would bring up divorce in the women's rights convention in 1860. Lucy Stone agreed with them. She wrote, "I am glad you will speak on the divorce question, provided you yourself are clear on the subject. It is a great grave topic that one shudders to grapple, but its hour is coming. . . . God touch your lips if you speak on it."

But when Susan urged the convention to work for better divorce laws for women, "consternation spread through the . . . convention." Antoinette Brown

Blackwell, the first woman ordained as a minister, and a leader of the women's movement, spoke against Susan. Marriage, she said, "must be lifelong." Other important people spoke against Susan's ideas. One of them was Reverend A. D. Mayo, an abolitionist who had also supported Susan's efforts for women. He said to Susan, "You are not married. You have no business to be discussing marriage." Susan replied, "Well Mr. Mayo, you are not a slave. Suppose you quit lecturing on slavery."

It was a smart answer, but smart answers would not be enough. With many women opposed to reforming the divorce laws, there would be a hard struggle ahead.

This drawing shows young women at a college graduation party in about 1890, when women were beginning to attend college in considerable numbers. The men are looking morose because there is nothing to drink but tea.

Divorce was not Susan's only concern. She had had a good education for the time, and she believed that girls should be educated as well as boys. In fact, she believed that boys and girls ought to go to school together. Sometimes they did, but, especially in the higher grades, they were taught separately. Susan believed that they should be together in the classroom so that the two sexes could get to know each other better. Undoubtedly she believed that if girls were educated in the same classroom with boys, they would quickly learn that they were just as smart as boys.

Yet another interest of Susan's was the difference in wages for men and women. Almost always women were paid less than men for doing the same job. It had happened to Susan as a schoolteacher, and she had not liked it. But it was a much worse situation for the millions of women working in big-city factories. Females from poor families often worked in terrible conditions in factories for wages that were hardly enough to live on. Many of them were teenagers, and some of them were girls of ten or twelve years old. The money they earned was barely enough for food and the cheapest clothes. There was little left for fun.

All of these problems for women troubled her, but more and more she saw that if women could have control of their money, they could solve some of their difficulties. In 1848—by chance at the time of the Seneca Falls Convention—the New York State Assembly had passed a law giving women some property rights. It had not gone far enough though. Susan now thought that something more could be done. She realized that many wealthy men gave money or land to their daughters. When the daughters got married, the husbands took charge of the money and in many cases wasted it. These wealthy fathers might support a law letting their daughters keep the money given to them.

In 1860 Susan spent the winter in Albany, the capital of New York. Day after day she called on legislators to talk to them about the "married woman's property laws." As the new law was coming to a vote, she decided that Elizabeth Stanton must give a strong speech to the Assembly. She was sure that Elizabeth, using Susan's facts and figures, could write a convincing speech.

Susan went back to Seneca Falls, where Elizabeth still lived. She poured out to Elizabeth all the facts and figures she had gathered about the ways in which reckless husbands had wasted their wives' property. She then looked after Elizabeth's many children while Elizabeth shut herself in her room to write her speech. By now the Stanton children knew Susan well and called

In the latter half of the nineteenth century and well into the twentieth century, millions of women were employed in factories with bad conditions and very low pay. This picture shows workers, many of them teenagers or even younger girls, entering a textile factory.

her Aunt Susan. She cooked for them, washed them, kept them in line with her firm discipline while Elizabeth wrote the speech.

In March 1860 Susan and Elizabeth went back to Albany. Elizabeth gave the speech to the Assembly. It was rare for a woman to give an important speech to the Assembly. The galleries were packed. At the end the applause was long. The next day the Assembly passed the Married Women's Property Bill. Women in New York State could keep any money they earned, could own property, could make contracts. It was a great victory for women's rights.

Chapter 4

SETBACKS

THE 1850S HAD BEEN A GOOD TIME for the women's movement. First there had been the convention in Seneca Falls in 1848, which had awakened many women to the possibilities for change. In the early 1850s Susan B. Anthony and Elizabeth Cady Stanton had started working together. They had soon pulled other determined women in with them, like Lucy Stone and Lucretia Mott. Also important to the leadership of the women's movement

Susan B. Anthony in about 1885. She was much sterner than Elizabeth in her appearance and always wore proper clothes, but in person she was often warm, intelligent, and funny.

were Ernestine Rose—an immigrant who shocked even reformers with some of her opinions—and Antoinette Brown Blackwell, the female minister.

With these people, the women's movement now had solid leadership. And by the mid-1850s Susan had come to be seen as the most important of them all. She was not the best speaker, Elizabeth Stanton was that. But Susan had the sharpest political mind. She could always figure out what had to be done next—what sort of petitions to get up, where and when to hold the next conference, which men might be useful to the movement.

She was also always careful to do her "homework"— to look up the facts and figures, to get all possible information. She was well-informed and always had a good, logical answer to her opponents.

Perhaps most important, Susan, more than any of the rest, was unwilling to compromise, to back down. She saw how women were being wronged, and what rights they ought to have. She would then push fearlessly ahead, regardless of who was against her. She had great moral authority. People knew that she was honest and just, and they found themselves willing to go along with her.

However, by the late 1850s the women's movement was facing a problem Susan and the others had not

Although the women's movement attracted much attention in nineteenth-century America, far more contentious was the movement to end slavery and then to give freed blacks their civil rights. This picture shows the famous abolitionist speaker Wendell Phillips giving an antislavery speech in Boston, where there was much concern for the cause.

expected. In America there had always been some opposition to slavery, mostly in the North. But the opposition had been growing through the 1850s, and by the end of the decade the country was beginning to split down the middle over the question of abolition. It was *the* big issue. For many people, perhaps the majority in both the North and the South, it was the *only* issue.

Susan and others in the women's movement were opposed to slavery. Freedom, they believed, was the right of all Americans. Did not the Declaration of Independence call for the right to life, liberty, and the pursuit of happiness for all, not just for white males?

But now they discovered that the men in the abolitionist movement wanted them to drop their demands for women's rights. The women's movement would have to be put on hold until the slaves got their freedom. Susan did not especially like the idea. It seemed to her that the rights of the female half of the population were just as important as the rights of African Americans, who were far smaller in number. Half of blacks, she pointed out, were women.

But abolitionists said that the cruelty endured by slaves was far worse than any pain a well-fed woman living in a comfortable home suffered. Of course a

A painting of an antislavery convention in 1840, when the abolitionist movement was beginning to grow. As the picture shows, only a small number of women attended such meetings. Only the men spoke.

great many women were working in factories at low wages and were not well fed or living in comfortable homes. Nonetheless, Susan had to agree that they were not treated as cruelly as black slaves were.

Then, in 1861 the great Civil War tore the nation apart. Women in both the North and the South had to put all their efforts into the war, whichever side they were on. The women's movement was set aside.

In 1865 the Civil War ended. Soon the government set about changing the Constitution to give African Americans their rights. Susan, Elizabeth, and others believed that women, too, ought to be given their rights at the same time as blacks got theirs. Hadn't the men promised that once blacks were free, the women's turn would come?

To their shock and horror they discovered that the women were to be shoved aside once more. The male leaders of the abolitionists said that they could not push for rights for blacks and women at the same time. There was still much feeling in the United States against both black's rights and women's rights. Giving the vote to women, some men said, would set husband and wife against each other and make every home a "hell on earth." If they tried for both at once, neither would get passed. "It is the Negro's hour," the abolitionists said.

Susan took a close look at the changes to the Constitution the men wanted, set out in the proposed Fourteenth Amendment to the Constitution. The first section of it was agreeable to the women's movement. It said, basically, that "all persons born or naturalized in the United States" were citizens, and should have the rights and privileges of citizens. But the second part of the Fourteenth Amendment said flatly that the vote would go only to "male inhabitants." Elizabeth Stanton, who was also studying the proposed Fourteenth Amendment wrote to Susan that they must do something. "Women's cause is in deep water. . . . There is pressing need of our women's rights convention."

At the time Elizabeth had moved into a new home in New York City, where her husband had taken a job. She urged Susan to stay with her to make plans. "I hope in a short time to be comfortably located in a new house where we will have a room ready for you. . . . I long to put my arms about you once more and hear you scold me for all my sins and shortcomings. . . . Yes, our work is one, and we are one in aim and sympathy and should be together. Come home."

As it happened, people trying to get rights for African Americans were having a convention in New York that summer of 1867. Susan and Elizabeth

This cartoon shows George Washington seated between Elizabeth and Susan. Actually, it is very doubtful that Washington would have supported a women's movement in his own day.

decided that there ought not to be two conventions, one for black's rights and one for women's rights. Instead there ought to be one Equal Rights convention to fight for both groups of people.

But the male leaders of the black rights group refused. In a debate over the matter the famous editor Horace Greeley, whom Susan knew well, said, "Help us get the word 'white' out of the Constitution. . . . Your turn will come." To clinch his argument he said, "If you vote, are you ready to fight?"

Susan replied, "Yes, Mr. Greeley, just as you fought in the late war [Civil War]—at the point of a goose quill [pen]." She went on to point out that hundreds of women had fought in that war, disguised as men. They were never paid for their service, but rather were discharged in disgrace when they were discovered.

But no argument the women made did any good. The new amendments to the Constitution gave the vote to male blacks but not to females of any race.

Susan could see that the fight would be longer and harder than she had expected.

She now decided that the women's movement had been scattering its shots too widely. Women had been fighting for the property act, for changes in the divorce law, for better education, and for the right to enter business. They wanted opportunities in professions like law, the ministry, and medicine. They must now concentrate on one thing. That should be women's suffrage—the vote. That, Susan believed, came before everything else. If women had the vote, they could force male politicians to listen to them and take their ideas and feelings seriously. Indeed, with the vote, women could run for public office and help to make new laws. Without the power of the vote, politicians could go on ignoring women. So in 1869 she and Elizabeth founded a new organization, the National Woman Suffrage Association.

Unhappily, their old comrade in the fight, Lucy Stone, along with some other well-known feminists, were upset by the strong stands on various issues that Susan and Elizabeth were taking. They believed that more could be gained if women moved more softly and cautiously. They felt that Susan had "a lust for power" and that Elizabeth was "too radical." So they formed their own organization, which they called the American

Woman Suffrage Association. The next twenty-odd years the two organizations would work separately.

Susan decided to move to Washington D.C., where she began to regularly meet with congressmen and other powerful men to urge them to support women's rights. She had no family to care for and was the person most experienced in the ins and outs of daily politics. She knew which congressmen were sympathetic to her cause, and which ones were opposed. She knew when bills of importance to women were being debated in Congress, and the states that might be ready to consider the issue.

However, she was away from Washington frequently. For some time she had recognized that westerners were more open to new ideas than easterners were. Out on the Great Plains, in the Northwest, and the Southwest, Americans were creating new villages, towns, and whole states from scratch. It was "a land of new beginnings." Might it not also be a land of new beginnings for women?

Susan now traveled more than ever. If travel in the East had sometimes been difficult, in the West it was far worse. There were, of course, no airplanes. The great train network we have today was still being built. In northern areas, winter snows could halt trains for days.

Travel, especially in the West, was rough and risky in Susan's time. She often had difficulty getting to the small towns where she wanted to speak. The photograph shows an engine of the Utah Central Railroad on a crude wooden bridge.

Sometimes she was forced to travel by stagecoach, by horse and buggy, or even by oxcart. Once she wrote:

> *I have been on tours for four months, sometimes without the luxury of a cup of coffee in a private home. [Susan liked her regular cup of coffee.] Once I was traveling for six months without a home-cooked meal. One gets very tired of mediocre hotels and state depot dining rooms.*

Another time she took a stagecoach through the mountains in Colorado.

> *. . . the ride down that mountain pass, "Slum Gullion" they call it, was the most fearful rough and tumble I ever experienced . . . even here, in this deep ravine, just wide enough for the Gunnison River and one street on its bank, the height is still 8,500 feet. All that fearfully long, but beautiful, frosty night, the moon shone brightly and on scenery most magnificent. At midnight I alighted at Wagon Wheel Gap, and with tin cup in hand trudged through the sand to the Rio Grande bank, bound to drink fresh from the pure, cold waters from the snow peaks above.*

There were often accidents.

> *I am now over one hundred miles on my stage-route south, and horrible indeed are the roads—miles and miles of corduroy (logs laid across the earth) and then twenty miles of [mud]—heavy clay without a particle of loam and rolls up on the wheels until rim, spokes, and hub are one solid circle. The wheels cease to turn and actually slide over the ground, and then driver and men passengers jump out and with chisels and shingles cut the clay off the wheels.*

But she was indomitable. She would not give up. In particular, she liked going to small, out-of-the-way places. It was hard to get to such little towns and villages, but she knew that people there would come out to hear her talk, because they had nothing better to do, especially during long, boring winters.

All this travel paid off, for she began to have victories in the West. During this time the areas that are now the states of Wyoming and Utah were called territories. They were not yet states, but were still under the control of the national government in Washington. However, they were getting ready to be states, and the people who lived in these and other territories were allowed to have their own governments, up to a point.

A drawing, probably from a magazine, of women preparing to vote in Cheyenne, Wyoming, in 1888, soon after the territory granted suffrage to women. Even after they got the vote, a lot of women felt uneasy about it, fearful that it was not feminine to vote. It took some courage for women to go to the polls.

In 1869 the Wyoming Territory passed laws giving women the vote, the right to serve on juries, and to be elected to government offices. Married women were given property rights. Utah and then some other territories did the same.

With these victories Susan sensed that the tide was finally turning. Surely other states, when they saw that the votes of women in Wyoming did not damage men or marriage, would be ready to give women the vote. But Susan was wrong.

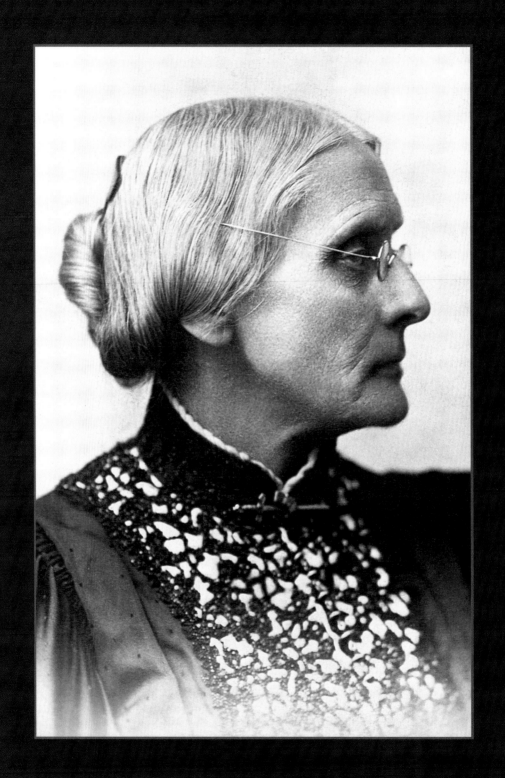

Chapter 5

AN UPHILL BATTLE

To Susan B. Anthony and others involved in the battle for women's rights, the fight seemed to go on endlessly. They had started with high hopes many years before. Surely any sensible person could see that women ought to be able to vote, to have money and property of their own, to divorce a cruel husband. By 1870, when the fight over the Fourteenth Amendment was lost, Susan was fifty and Elizabeth Stanton was fifty-five.

Susan B. Anthony in 1895, when she was seventy-five years old. She would go on leading the women's movement for another five years.

But it never occurred to them to give up. They had fought for twenty years, and they would fight for another twenty if necessary. It turned out that even another twenty years would not be enough.

But however slowly, they were gaining ground. Women who had been children when Susan started the battle were now growing up. Ideas that had seemed strange and foreign in the 1840s were becoming accepted. Remember how shocked people were when Susan first tried to speak at conventions? By the 1870s it was taken for granted that women could not only speak but hold conventions of their own.

Nonetheless, the vote seemed a long way off. Susan cast about for ideas. What about the Fourteenth Amendment? Didn't it say that "All persons born . . . in the United States" were citizens and entitled to the "privileges" of citizens. Wasn't the right to vote a privilege of a citizen? If the Constitution said she had a right to vote, she would.

In fact, the year before, two other women had voted, claiming their right under the Fourteenth Amendment. In November 1872 Susan persuaded several women to go with her to register as voters. (In most cases voters must register ahead of time.) The inspector in charge told Susan that under New York

Neither Susan nor Elizabeth lived to see women get the vote. The fight was carried on by younger women until victory in 1920. Here a suffragette speaks to a crowd, mostly men, probably not long before 1920.

State law she could not register to vote. Susan replied that she was voting under rights given in the Fourteenth Amendment. Of course national law overrides state laws. The inspector stammered and then discussed it with other inspectors. In the end he gave in and registered Susan and the other women.

Susan was by this time a very well-known person. Whenever she did anything important there was an uproar in the newspapers. The papers ran big stories about Susan registering to vote. One pointed out that anyone who voted illegally had committed a crime and was liable to a $500 fine and three years in jail.

Despite this, Susan soon persuaded fifty other women to register. On election day, November 5, 1872, Susan voted. She wrote Elizabeth, "Well, I have gone and done it!! . . . Not a jeer not a word—not a look—disrespectful has met a single woman."

Susan hoped that across the country millions of women would follow her example. However, they did not. The idea of actually breaking the law to vote troubled most women. The uproar in the press continued. A few weeks later a United States marshal rang Susan's doorbell. He handed her papers charging her with the crime of voting.

The marshal was very embarrassed at having to arrest this famous lady. He told Susan that she could come down to his office whenever it was convenient. Susan insisted on being arrested immediately. She wanted to keep the issue hot in people's minds. She also wanted to force a trial to see what a jury would decide. She held out her hands for the handcuffs. The marshal refused to handcuff her, but he guided her out of the house and onto a streetcar. Soon the conductor came along and asked for her fare. She said, "I'm traveling at the expense of the government. This gentleman is escorting me to jail. Ask him for my fare."

The trial took place in June 1873. According to Susan and Elizabeth in a book the latter wrote:

On the bench sat Judge Hunt, a small-brained, pale-faced, prim-looking man, enveloped in a faultless suit of black broadcloth, and a snowy white necktie. This was the first criminal case he had been called on to try since his appointment, and with remarkable forethought he had penned his decision before hearing it.

So it was. Susan's lawyer made the argument that Susan was entitled to vote under the Fourteenth Amendment. The prosecutor gave his side of it. But Judge Hunt, instead of letting the jury consider the case, told them to find Susan guilty. Susan's lawyer immediately asked that the jury be allowed to state their opinions. Judge Hunt said no, and dismissed the jury. The trial was over.

Susan was fined $100. Susan said that she would never pay the fine, and she never did. Two of the unfortunate men who had allowed her to vote went to jail for five days. However, the women who had voted brought them home-cooked meals each night they were in jail.

The trial made news all over the United States. More and more, people were asking themselves what

Susan, just before she retired to make room for younger women. She continued to dress in the most proper clothes and sit ramrod straight.

was wrong with letting women vote. Increasing numbers were saying that it would be a good thing if women voted. The reform movements that had started when Susan was a girl had been growing in strength year by year. Americans were drinking less than they used to. More people were going regularly to church. Spitting was not so frequent. Pigs and dogs no longer wandered into churches. In general, the idea was spreading that people ought not to be looking out for themselves first, but should try to consider the needs of their families, their communities, and their nation. In the opinion of many, the United States was becoming a better place.

It seemed clear enough that women, some famous, most of them unknown, had played a big role in changing things. Women had been important in the temperance movement, important in making life in America more "decent." It seemed to many people that the more influence women had, the better the nation would become. It would therefore be a good idea to let them vote, for they would vote for candidates who wanted reform.

By 1885 seventeen states had given women the right to vote for school boards, the idea being that women ought to have a say in how their children were educated. More and more, Susan saw that the best chance for victories was in the western states. But even there the opposition was very strong. Many men did not like seeing women become powerful, whether through the vote or anything else. The liquor interests, such as people who bottled beer, wine, and whiskey, along with owners of saloons, didn't want women to have the vote. They feared they would vote for temperance. Many politicians didn't want women to vote, for fear that they would vote them out of office. In 1882 woman suffrage lost in Nebraska. It won the next year, but the enemies fought it in the courts.

During these years many of the western territories were being admitted as states. Each time that happened, the territory's constitution had to be approved by Congress. If that territory had woman suffrage, Congress could turn it down for statehood.

The Wyoming Territory came up for statehood in 1889. It had had woman suffrage for twenty years, but now Congress thought perhaps it should not admit Wyoming until it denied women the right to vote.

Susan listened to the debates in Congress with growing despair. Was the battle the women had won twenty years before to be lost? Soon it became clear that Congress would go against woman suffrage in Wyoming. Then, just as the decision was to be made, there came a message from the Wyoming legislature. It said, "We will remain out of the Union a hundred years rather than come in without suffrage." Congress gave in.

Progress was painfully slow, but it was being made. One historian says, "Woman suffrage was becoming respectable in the West, and a woman was no longer ostracized by her friends for working with Susan B. Anthony." She was, in fact, wearing down her opponents.

In the year Wyoming came into the Union with woman suffrage, Susan was seventy years old. She still

Elizabeth and Susan in 1885. They remained the closest of friends even though as time passed Elizabeth grew less able to help with their work due to ill health.

had a lot of energy, still traveled endlessly to speak for the cause of women. But she knew that there was a long road ahead for women's rights. She believed that she might not live to see the day when women all across America could vote.

It was therefore important for her to leave the women's movement in good shape. She must bring in younger leaders. One she had a high opinion of was Carrie Chapman Catt, who had worked on the campaign for the vote in South Dakota. Carrie had graduated from Iowa State College and had studied law briefly. She was married, but that had not stopped her from working for woman suffrage. Susan saw good things in Carrie. She put her in charge of the campaign to win the vote in Colorado. And in 1893, under Carrie's energetic leadership, Colorado voted in favor of woman suffrage. Susan now gave Carrie more responsibility.

Carrie Chapman Catt was an example of how far women had traveled since Susan's youth. Then it had been almost impossible for a woman to go to college and entirely impossible for her to study law. Carrie had done both. The women's movement now had in it many young women with college degrees and other kinds of training. These women felt strongly that the women's movement should not be divided between Susan's group and Lucy Stone's. They pressed Susan and Lucy to merge their organizations, and they did. Many of the younger women wanted Susan to be president of the new organization, but Susan insisted that

Elizabeth be elected. She was, but she was beginning to suffer from health problems, and Susan soon became the leader.

Susan had always run things with a firm hand. So respected was she by younger women that they did not object to being guided by her. But Susan understood that they were beginning to grow restless. They wanted more say in things. Susan knew she must relax that firm hand. The important thing was for her to see that the right people took over from her—people with the strength, courage, and intelligence to keep the fight going. Finally she told her younger companions that she would retire in 1900, when she would be eighty. It was time to pass the torch.

Members of the International Council of Women

Susan had great faith in Carrie Chapman Catt who had done important work to win the vote for women in Colorado. She arranged for Carrie to take over when Susan retired. Carrie lived until 1947 and saw women not only gain the vote, but make great strides in other ways as well.

She wanted Carrie Chapman Catt to take over. At the 1900 convention of the organization, now called the National American Woman Suffrage Association, Carrie was elected president. One biographer describes the moment:

Carrie Chapman Catt, at forty-one about half Anthony's age, was easily elected, 254-24. When the results were announced, the delegates and others burst into applause. Then, as the realization sank in that the woman who had guided and inspired them for half a century would no longer be in charge, a profound silence blanketed the hall. Against the background of a few muffled sobs in the audience, the business of the convention proceeded. Eyewitnesses were in awe.

In 1914 the battle for the vote was far from sure. Here women campaign in New York City from their own information office.

Neither Susan B. Anthony nor Elizabeth Cady Stanton lived to see their life's work completed. Elizabeth died in 1902. Susan died on March 13, 1906. But the movement they had driven forward marched on, and in 1920 the United States of America finally gave all women the vote.

If Susan did not live to see this moment, she did see much else. Women were going to college in greater and greater numbers. Women could, largely, control their own money and other property. They could more easily divorce abusive husbands and keep their children. Women were beginning to get jobs in industry, not just as mill workers on the factory floor, but in offices as well. Women were organizing their own labor unions. A great deal had improved for women, and much was owed to Susan B. Anthony. The place of women in America today was built on the foundation she laid. This is what she had hoped for and worked for her entire life. She once said, "I look for the day when the woman who has a political or judicial brain will have as much right to sit on the Supreme Bench or in the Senate as . . . men have now. . . . And this time will come."

In her last public appearance she looked around at the women who were working with her and said, "With such women consecrating their lives, failure is impossible." She was right, and those words are still a slogan for feminists a hundred years after she spoke them.

With the vote finally won in 1920, feminist leaders were determined that women should use their votes to improve American society. This campaigner holds an umbrella over her child as she displays her sign.

TIME LINE

1820 February 15: Susan Brownell Anthony is born in Adams, Massachusetts.

1851 Susan meets Elizabeth Cady Stanton for the first time in Syracuse, New York.

1854 Anthony starts to petition for married women's property rights. She begins her New York State campaign for woman's right to vote.

1869 Anthony calls for the first Woman Suffrage Convention in Washington, D.C.

1872 Susan is arrested for voting.

1906 March 13: Susan B. Anthony dies at the age of eighty-six.

1920 The 19th Amendment to the U.S. Constitution grants the right to vote to all women over age twenty-one.

Author's Note on Sources

There are several good biographies of Susan B. Anthony. The most recent is *Susan B. Anthony: A Biography of a Singular Feminist*, by Kathleen Barry (NYU Press: New York, 1988). Also useful is an older book, *Susan B. Anthony: Rebel, Crusader, Humanitarian*, by Alma Lutz (Beacon Press: Boston, 1959). *Elizabeth Cady Stanton: A Radical for Women's Rights*, by Lois W. Banner (Little, Brown: Boston, 1980) will round out the picture. Also valuable is *Failure Is Impossible*, edited by Lynn Sherr (Times Books: New York, 1995), a collection of Anothony's writings and speeches.

For students there is *Susan B. Anthony*, by Barbara Weisberg (Chelsea House: Pennsylvania, 1988).

INDEX

Phillips, Wendell, *49*
portraits/photographs of
   Susan B. Anthony, *4, 14, 18,
   20, 32, 40, 46, 60, 65, 66, 69*
property rights of women, 23,
   44–45, 59

Quakers, 10, 11

Reform movements, 26, 67
Rochester, New York, 19, 30
Rose, Ernestine, 48

Seneca Falls, New York, 19,
   28, 31
Smith, Ann, 26
Smith, Gerrit, 26
Sons of Temperance, 37
speaking out, 16, 18, 36,
   38–39, 62
Stanton, Elizabeth Cady, 19,
   20, 21–31, *28*, 36, 44, 48,
   52, 54, *69*
Stanton, Henry Brewster,
   26–28
Stone, Lucy, *35*, 35–36, 41,
   54, 70

suffrage, 29, 37, 54, *59*,
   68–69. *see also* vote, right to
suffragettes, 7, *9*, *63*, *73*

Teaching career, 13–14
temperance movement,
   15–16, *17*, 25, *25*, *36*, 67
travel, 55–58

Vote, right to, 29, 51, 53, 59,
   62–63, 67, *73*, 75. *see also*
   suffrage

Wages, equal, 43
Washington, D. C., 55
Willard, Emma, 23
Woman Suffrage Convention,
   76
women's rights conventions,
   27, 29–30, 37, 41, 44
women's rights movement,
   31, 36, 40, 48–55, 70
words of Susan B. Anthony, 7,
   13, 15, 34, 35, 38, 42, 53,
   56, 57, 58, 64, 65, 74, 75
Wyoming Territory, 59, 68–69

ABOUT THE AUTHOR

James Lincoln Collier has written many books, both fiction and nonfiction, for children and adults. His interests span history, biography, and historical fiction. He is an authority on the history of jazz and performs weekly on the trombone in New York City.

My Brother Sam Is Dead was named a Newbery Honor Book and a Jane Addams Honor Book and was a finalist for a National Book Award. *Jump Ship to Freedom* and *War Comes to Willy Freemen* were each named a notable Children's Trade Book in the Field of Social Studies by the National Council for Social Studies and the Children's Book Council. Collier received the Christopher Award for *Decision in Philadelphia: The Constitutional Convention of 1787*. He lives in Pawling, New York.